DALMATIANS

FAVORITE DOG BREEDS

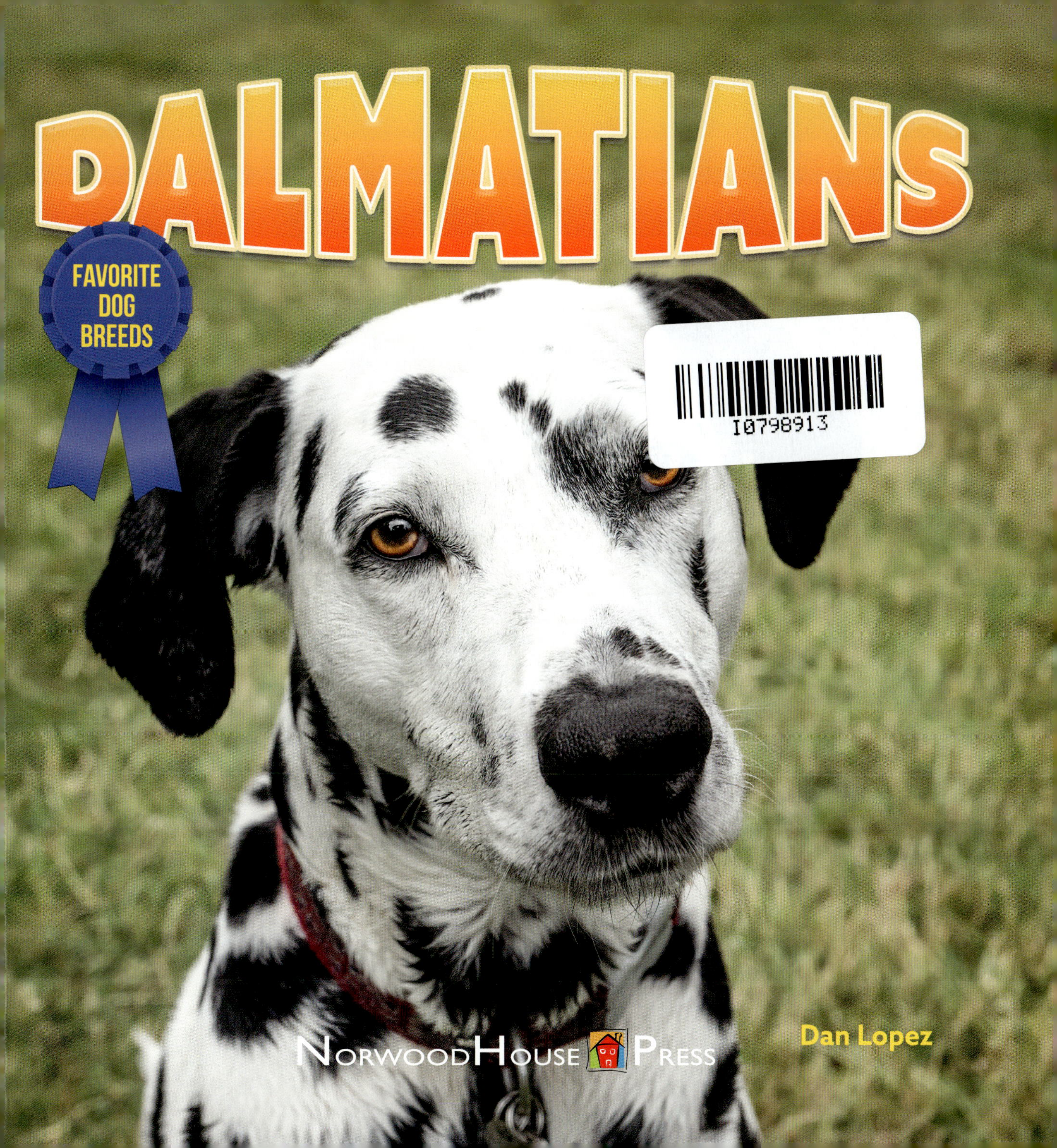

I0798913

Dan Lopez

NorwoodHouse Press

Cataloging-in-Publication Data

Names: Lopez, Dan.
Title: Dalmatians / Dan Lopez.
Description: Buffalo, NY : Norwood House Press, 2026. | Series: Favorite dog breeds| Includes glossary and index.
Identifiers: ISBN 9781978576599 (pbk.) | ISBN 9781978576605 (library bound) | ISBN 9781978576612 (ebook)
Subjects: LCSH: Dalmatian dog--Juvenile literature.
Classification: LCC SF429.D3 L67 2026 | DDC 636.72--dc23

Published in 2026 by
Norwood House Press
2544 Clinton Street
Buffalo, NY 14224

Copyright © 2026 Norwood House Press
Designer: Rhea Magaro
Editor: Kim Thompson

Photo credits: Cover, p. 1 chrisukphoto, Giraphics/Shutterstock.com; p. 4 Wikipedia.com; p. 5 Fran Estevez/Shutterstock.com; p. 6 chrisukphoto/Shutterstock.com; p. 7 Bianca Grueneberg/Shutterstock.com; p. 8 Jason.H/Shutterstock.com; p. 9 Amy Richmond/Shutterstock.com; p. 10 Waldir-WFC/Shutterstock.com; p. 11, 13 Library of Con-gress/Shutterstock.com; p. 15 Jeremy Liebman/Shutterstock.com; p. 16 Nina Buday/Shutterstock.com; p. 17 chrisukphoto/Shutterstock.com; p. 18 Anton Pentegov/Shutterstock.com; p. 21 sergey kolesnikov/Shutterstock.com

All rights reserved. No part of this book may be reproduced in any form without permission in writing from the publisher, except by a reviewer.

Printed in the United States of America

Some of the images in this book illustrate individuals who are models. The depictions do not imply actual situations or events.

CPSIA compliance information: Batch #CWNHP26: For further information contact Norwood House Press at 1-800-237-9932.

Find us on

TABLE OF CONTENTS

Meet the Dalmatian

Dalmatians are popular pets. Dogs of this **breed** are known for their dark spots and their history of helping firefighters.

Dalmatians star in the Disney movie *101 Dalmatians*.

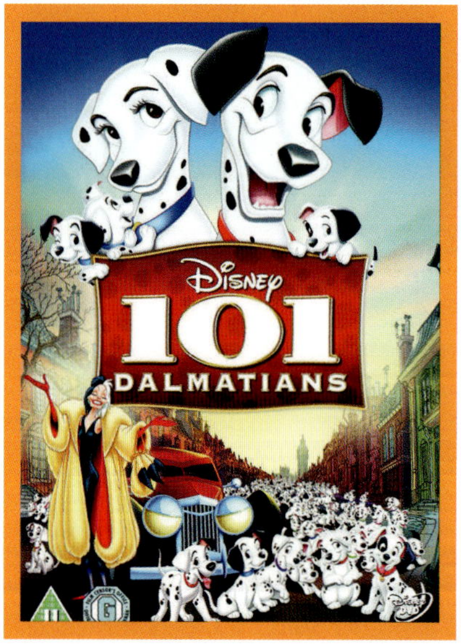

What Do Dalmatians Look Like?

Dalmatians are thin and **muscular**. Adults can stand 24 inches (60 centimeters) tall. They can weigh up to 70 pounds (32 kilograms).

A Dalmatian's short ears droop down. Its tail is long and skinny.

Dalmatians have short, white fur that is thick and **glossy**. They are covered with black or dark brown spots. They even have spots in their mouths and on the bottoms of their paws!

When puppies are born, they are all white.
Their spots come in a few weeks later.

Where Do Dalmatians Come From?

Dalmatians were probably first raised in Dalmatia. This region is now part of the European country Croatia.

Long ago, people noticed that Dalmatians made good **companions** for horses. The dogs ran beside horse-drawn carriages. These "coach dogs" protected horses and riders from robbers.

Once, firefighters used pumper wagons pulled by horses. Dalmatians ran with the horses and kept them calm. They helped clear a path so the wagon could get to the fire quickly.

ROYAL FIRE CO

Today, many fire stations still have pet Dalmatians. These **mascots** keep the firefighters company. They may ride in fire trucks. Some have names like Hydrant or Chief.

SL13004T
N.Y.
FDNY

Do Dalmatians Make Good Pets?

Dalmatians make great pets. They are smart and **affectionate**.

These dogs love games and activities. They are always ready to play!

Dalmatians are **loyal** to their families. They will bark at strangers. They make good **watchdogs**.

What Do Dalmatians Need?

Dalmatians are **agile** and **energetic**. They need at least two hours of daily exercise. Good training can help them learn when to play and when to be calm.

Glossary

affectionate (uh-FEK-shuh-nit): loving and caring

agile (AJ-il): able to move quickly and easily

breed (breed): one type or kind of an animal

companions (kuhm-PAN-yuhnz): friends, buddies, or partners

energetic (en-ur-JET-ik): strong, active, and full of energy

glossy (GLAW-see): shiny

loyal (LOI-uhl): faithful and true to someone or something

mascots (MAS-kahts): symbols, especially animals, that represent teams and that are supposed to bring good luck

muscular (MUHS-kyuh-lur): having strong muscles

watchdogs (WAHCH-dawgs): dogs kept to guard property

Thinking Questions

1. Describe a Dalmatian's fur.

2. What were "coach dogs"?

3. How have Dalmatians helped firefighters throughout history?

4. Why do Dalmatians make good watchdogs?

5. Why do Dalmatians need lots of exercise?

Index

About the Author

Dan Lopez is a writer who loves dogs! He has a German shepherd named Hans and an Irish setter named Tam. They love to go for walks in the woods together. Sometimes, they jump in the lake for a swim. Dan lives in Indiana with his wife and three kids.